DAN FOR DINNER

Published by Baker Books
A division of Baker Publishing Group
P.O. Box 6287, Grand Rapids, MI 49516-6287
www.bakerbooks.com

First Edition

Printed in the United States of America

Library of Congress Cataloging-in-Publication Data
Names: Blair, Brett, author. | Koenig, James, illustrator.
Title: Dan for dinner / Brett Cameron Blair ; illustrated by James Koenig.
Description: Grand Rapids, MI : Baker Books, A division of Baker Publishing Group, 2018.
  | Series: Creator's toy chest | Includes bibliographical references and index. | Audience:
  Ages 3–7.
Identifiers: LCCN 2017030032 | ISBN 9780801017247 (cloth)
Subjects: LCSH: Daniel (Biblical figure)—Juvenile literature. | Bible stories, English—Daniel.
Classification: LCC BS580.D2 B59 2018 | DDC 224.5092—dc23
LC record available at https://lccn.loc.gov/2017030032

Published in association with the literary agency D.C. Jacobson & Associates, an Author Management Company, www.dcjacobson.com.

18 19 20 21 22 23 24   7 6 5 4 3 2 1

THE
CREATOR'S
TOY CHEST

DAN FOR DINNER

• Daniel's Story •

Brett Blair

Illustrated by James Koenig

BakerBooks

a division of Baker Publishing Group
Grand Rapids, Michigan

• • •

To Brett
The Wise

• • •

Down in the dungeon dark and deep
A den of lions growl and sleep.

Up in the palace a prophet named Dan
Speaks to the king about God's plan.

Out in the courtyard all the king's men
Plot to throw Dan down in the den.

And as they plot

The king says, "Dan, I had a dream,
The craziest thing I've ever seen."

"A towering tree stood
In the middle of the land,
The fruit abundant,
The red leaves grand.
The animals found shelter.
The birds made nests.
All who found it, in it, found rest."

"In the sky an angel appeared,
And in my heart I deeply feared,
For out of the branches flew the birds
As the angel spoke these frightening words:

'Strip the leaves and scatter the fruit
But save the stump and spare the root.
Cut it down so animals flee.
Remove the glory from the tree.'"

"Dan, now you know what I have seen.
Can you tell me what it means?"

"You are the tree, Your Majesty.
Your kingdom's glory all can see.
But you do not do what good kings do,
And now the ax must cut you through.
From your head the crown will fall,
And you will leave this hallowed hall."

"You'll lose your power, then your mind.
You'll live like beasts and not mankind.
Like an ox you'll eat the grass,
And seven years will have to pass
Till you admit the Lord Most High
Is King of kings under all the sky."

And so it happened as Dan had said.

The king went crazy and lost his head.

He left his throne, his kingdom too.

For seven years drenched in dew,

He ate the grass like an ox,
Made his bed in jagged rocks.
His hair grew long like eagles' feathers,
His skin as rough as worn-out leather.

The king remembered Dan's last words:

"With your lips you must confess
To help the poor and the oppressed.
Then your kingdom will return to you
As you do the good that good kings do.

Your tree will grow, your leaves will bloom,
The bird's return will lift the gloom.
The beasts again will find their rest
Beneath the tree that heaven blessed."

Time passed. A new king took the throne,
A man that Dan had never known.

Dan prayed to God both day and night.
He helped the king, did his job right.
The king put Dan in command
Over the kingdom and the land.

And things went well, for a time.

But sooner or later the clock will chime

And the good times turn.

Then you learn

That life is filled with bumps and curves

That shake you down and test your nerves.

All the king's men made a pact
To make poor Dan a lion's snack.

To the king they said, "You are great.
You should make a law and set a date.
The law should say for thirty days
In all the kingdom no one prays
To gods or man or anyone else.
They can only pray to the king himself."

They wrote the law, and then the king
He sealed it with his royal ring.

Dan went home, fell to his knees,
Gave thanks to God, and said, "God, please!
Give me patience and make me strong,
Help me forgive when I am wronged,
For enemies wait at my door.
I fear for what they have in store."

The king's men watched and spied,
Grinned devilish grins with beady little eyes.
Through Dan's window they saw him pray.
"Now we got him. Now he'll pay!
The lions are hungry. They've not been fed.
Dan is done. He's as good as dead."

They told the king, and he grieved,
For now he knew he'd been deceived.
He liked Dan, liked Dan a lot,
But a law's a law and a knot's a knot.
Their tricky dirty stinky plot
Put the king in a no-good terrible awful spot.

The king sentenced Dan to the den
Because of crooked evil jealous men.

They lowered Dan to the dungeon's floor.
"Dan for dinner!" the lions roared.

"Dan for dinner!
        Dan for lunch!
                Dan for breakfast!
                        And maybe for brunch!"

Through the darkness, Dan saw the eyes
And wondered if God heard his cries.
"Lord, I'm down here with these beasts.
I think they want to have a feast."

The biggest lion stood on his paws,
Big white teeth and massive jaws.

The lion licked his chops.

They stood eye to eye.

He circled slowly round.

"I think," Dan said, "I will die."

The lion sat. Then he lay down.
The big cat purred and wrapped Dan round.

Dan laid his head on the lion's mane.
They slept that night quiet and tame.

The king turned and tossed all night long.

That decree, he thought, *it is wrong.*

He ran to the dungeon at dawn's first light.

"Roll the stone. We'll see who's right."

The light streamed in, and Dan awoke.

The lion still wrapped him like a cloak.

"Dan? You down there? You all right?

The God whom you serve,

Did he save you tonight?"

The king's heart filled with a dreadful fear
When he heard a sound he did not want to hear.
Dan's lion growled, a loud fierce roar.
Laughing, Dan asked, "Do you need to say more?"

"Your Majesty," Dan yelled up to the king,
"I'm rested and ready if you'll throw down the sling."

The king jumped back and wiped his tears.
The joy in his heart banished his fears.

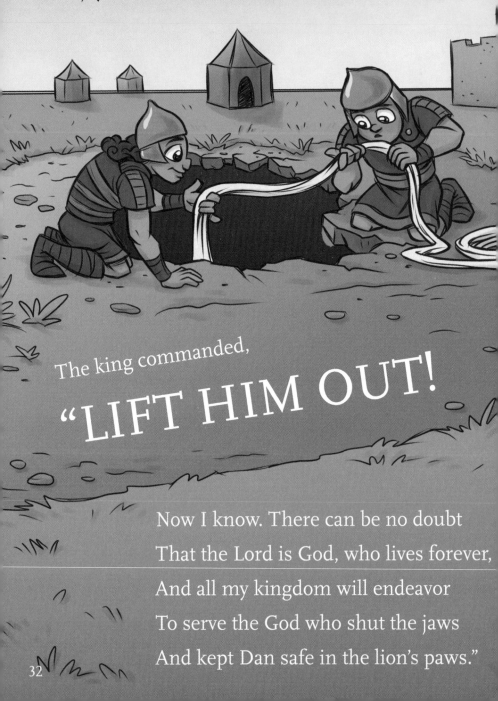

The king commanded,
"LIFT HIM OUT!

Now I know. There can be no doubt
That the Lord is God, who lives forever,
And all my kingdom will endeavor
To serve the God who shut the jaws
And kept Dan safe in the lion's paws."

All the king's men who tricked and lied
Were brought together and together tied.
When they were lowered
To the dungeon's floor,
"All the king's men!"
The lions ROARED.

"All the king's men for dinner!
All the king's men for lunch!
All the king's men for breakfast!
All the king's men for brunch!"